TERSE

NEESHANT SRIVASTAVA

Made with ♥ on the Notion Press Platform
www.notionpress.com

To the spirit of man.

Contents

1. NO BREAD NO WINE

Little as you are my son,
Jhony's Papa did say,
You wander the streets under the sun,
No women of wine or bread you may,
This journey is what the world has shunned.
You cannot hear me, my son,
I do not speak the common language,
I do see you polishing your gun,
This is not for the ages smeared in adage,
It needs to be done and if you want to run.
I don't foresee you getting close,
It's an uphill battle if you will,
Generations in fetters morose,
Not one will gather and kill,
The road too long and arduous.

2. ALL GOOD

What was that man that is old now,
What did he do when he was young,
The breeze still blows and the sun bows,
Before the night sprung,
With the night show.
What has he done,
When all his victories are gone,
And he sits frail and grey alone,
Young for good but ravaged to the bone,
That other man had miles to roam.
People shall forget,
For the past never existed,
And start again in a new hat,
Their voices gentler and crusted,
Not for long over the mumbling spat.

3. CLARA MY LOVE

Don't hide your eyes my love,

Clara your feminine fingers I see,

Morning in fits of yawn my love,

You need someone I see,

Did I kindle that flush on your cheeks my love.

Clara I am too cold I know,

For you to set off for far my love,

I can hear you call me I know,

As you sit there pretty at sundown for me my love,

Only to rub off the red and glow.

On those lips of sorrow and cheeks of rage,

But I cannot if you should know,

Come too close and rip off the cage,

Of what makes me before you bow,

Clara my love I shall suffer your umbrage.

4. MY PATH

My path the sound of creaks,
Like bells of failure,
Each time I fall and wake,
In another land and allure,
Of my true calling and make.
But God perchance my failures did see,
As he brought the unfinished seed,
Planted again for an evergreen tree
To not lament but proceed,
To the everlasting sea.
I rubbed my eyes again,
Pulled back and warned for the end,
But like a fool again,
I set off to mend,
Lost pride and disdain.

5. BACK HOME AGAIN

This home of ancient bricks,
Was a gift of my grandfather,
I grew up in this home and did stick,
Long after the world left for another,
From a city destitute and sick.
My father pushed me away,
To another far off land,
Where the world lay,
Where with the magic wand,
Dreams came true as they say.
I don't know why I came back,
To sickness and drought,
My home a worn-out wreck,
Sold to greed and bought,
Peace dawned on me and I was awake.

6. TICK, BOOM

Tick, boom, creak, sag,
Life up a leak of slush,
Indifferent world can't fix the snag,
As they hustle around the bush,
After the hidden fragrance of the stag.
Don't cry for them my son,
They will not come again,
To be the fugitive for the pun,
It's not too hard or in vain,
To walk the road and get it done.
Someone dimmed the lights my son,
And its too hard to see,
Frames gather dust unwon,
Music in coffins till debris,
Flowers without touch my son.

7. JET AGE

How things move at jet speed,
When the passing moment is obsolete,
Boys can't wait for the deed,
Girls flutter on the cheap street,
The earth longs for caress of feet.
Jonny was dead a long time ago,
His parents left him for the skies,
The jet age found him struggling slow,
They left him alone to lie,
Within his walls and hidden foes.
Jonny was silent and low,
Not manly enough for Cinderella,
Why he waited he did not know,
A fool for ages and a mania,
The sun did rise after the mighty blow,
For little Jonny, O! Anaemia.

8. A BOOK TO READ

Life is not a book to read,
How can paper set you free,
To sow one seed,
It takes a lifetime on bended knee,
For the sacred deed.
Look around to see,
Millions of animals in cages and chains,
Longing to own the key,
To be human again,
While humans are less than Holy.
This time will not come again,
Wasted lives will not be saved,
Ushered will be in disdain,
To lesser than rave,
Time is ticking insane.

9. LEAVES OF LOVE

Leaves of love often bitter,

They grow in the wild few,

Trample them by foot and the lose their glitter,

Till the time you finish your stew,

On a bright new day after the night saunter.

When did it happen your memory fails,

That woman or man in reams of veil,

Like love that just happens in no gust or gale,

Woman as far as that man like a seed that is sealed,

Will offer that last chance and if you fail…

Many then happened to come and go,

The man and his tryst with flesh,

While the woman felt a chivalrous bow,

The man and his lost love in the great rush,

While the woman with a different loyalty low.

What happened thus is for all of us to know.

PICTURE MS. RANDALL

Picture Ms. Randall,

She's crossed her hands low,

Big boys can afford a scandal,

As she stands in a sari with pedicured toes,

She's so white with a soft marble glow.

Some heathen eyes give her dirty looks,

She can't find the one for her,

The crowd of eyes and this stolen brook,

Can not the moment spur,
The brave one out of a fairy book.
For love happens without a sound,
And Ms. Randal is caught,
Between the loaf and coffee rounds,
The staff room of Senior high she sought,
Looks bare with just the hound,
Of loneliness and the missing plot.

10. TREASURE

He's got no mills running,
Or a fleet of ships to his name,
No one at his doorstep seeking,
A glimpse of a life in vain,
In a lost game of longings.
He may be down and out,
But not without a treasure trove,
Of gold and silver no doubt,
Of the sun and moon in their rove,
Of flowers of skin and birdies of rout.
Someone far away fell in love,
With this man of no name,
For some reason clear enough,
But she's not ready for the blame,
For his heart of pure up above.

11. EVERYTHING, BUT

Each one has a slice of something,
But not the whole fruit,
John has got a job, a house, a wife, going,
A life of fun like the man on the flute,
Yet deep in the night tossing and turning.
John gets up late in the morning,
To snatch his bag and run,
He is late again for something is burning,
His hands and feet did learn,
In a dark room to make a living.
Something has been left behind,
Too far now beyond a gaze,
To unlearn again and unwind,
To shut the sounds of haze,
John waits for the end.

12. UNTIL THE ANGELS

Know where you must go,
With empty pockets all alone,
Not a palace or a bow,
Suffering and weary to the bone,
Wait until the angels of snow.
Then you need not fear,
Or wander among the crowd,
Your life then is smooth as the river,
Your steps without a sound,
Your angel does hover.
Never be sad you man of sorrow,
You have done your part,
Get ready to leave 'morrow,
For the land of heart,
Don't doubt the angels or tarrow.

13. SOS

The young ones feel the heat,
A new generation and the same anxiety,
Gurus of penny repeat,
All that's been said in sobriety,
Like they know it and come discreet.
Voice of the ages is low,
The road is long but not lost,
To lead astray from the door,
Is a game for the great chaos,
For bits of heaven a constant allure.
No one seems to know,
The dancing devil from the divine,
As darkness grows thick on the moor,
Smiles die down and frowns line,
This age of fear and heart of sore.

14. CUBICLE MARTYR

Ron the young lad from lowland,
Comes to work in the city,
Gullible and clay for a command,
Work is fun around faces pretty,
He comes out smiling after much demand.
Ron the workaholic,
Says it's for the family,
Twenty-five years of mildew bricks,
In a packed cubicle lonely,
He has gone too far to come back.
Ron's youth of wine to the brim,
Of thick glasses and monster parties,
Holding women lascivious and trim,
Alone with sweet lips ala carte,
Way past midnight in hidden rooms.

15. ONE WHO CARES

Life your life and you shall find,
That no one cares or know your worth,
To sweeten the constant grind,
And want nothing back but heart,
Such ones are rare to find.
I walked by life through,
Laughed at and pushed off cliffs,
I searched for the someone true,
A broken heart and eyes never met as if,
I belonged to a different age to rue.
I finally found the one who cares,
After fifty autumns of gloom,
Her words were enough I declare,
To show her care in the August noon,
And find stones of solitaire.

www.ingramcontent.com/pod-product-compliance
Lightning Source LLC
Chambersburg PA
CBHW030512170726
47990CB00008BA/3164